# Contents

1  History and the National Curriculum     5

2  Planning a History Study Unit            9

3  Assessment                              11

4  Cross-curricular Links                  15

5  Guide to the Pupil Books                16

    The Romans                           17

    The Anglo-Saxons and Vikings         34

6  Resources                               51

7  Photocopiables                          53

# 1

# History and the National Curriculum

## Links between the ATs and Invaders and Settlers Study Unit

The ATs in History are likely to be the focus for all the investigations and tasks the children will carry out. The practical suggestions given below of links with the Invaders and Settlers core study unit illustrate this.

### Links with Attainment Target 1
**The development of the ability to describe and explain historical change and cause, and analyse different features of historical situations.**

#### Strand A: Change and Continuity
- Create a timeline of 1,000 years divided into centuries. Each Invader can be indicated by a different colour. See pages 32 and 53 for details.
- At the end of the study unit make a list of all the things that had remained the same, or changed in Britain, from 55 BC up to the death of Edward the Confessor.

#### Strand B: Causes and Consequences
- The causes and consequences of Alfred's victory over Guthrum in AD 878 can act as a useful focus for investigation.
- The causes of the success or failure of the 3 Roman invasions of Britain.

#### Strand C: Knowing about and understanding key features of past situations
- Compare the Viking technology of shipbuilding with a Roman galley for their suitability as invasion craft.
- Compare Roman villas with Anglo-Saxon houses.
- Make a display of life in a Roman town.

### Links with Attainment Target 2
**The development of the ability to understand interpretations of history.**
- Look at Tacitus' account of Boudica's revolt. Make maps of Boudica's movements and those of General Paulinus. Create role plays and write poems from either a Roman or a Celtic point of view.

## Links with Attainment Target 3

The development of pupil's ability to acquire evidence from historical sources, and form judgements about their reliability and value.

- Look at the different sources of evidence for Anglo-Saxon and Viking life - reconstructed Anglo-Saxon villages, artefacts from museums, sagas etc. Which sources were the most useful or reliable?

# The General Requirement and the Invaders and Settlers Study Unit

## Links with the Key Elements

### Political

- Britain as part of the Roman Empire and why the legions left.

### Economic, technological and scientific

- Viking raids and their long boats.

### Social

- The way of life of each of the invaders.

### Religious

- How each group of settlers became Christian.

### Cultural and aesthetic

- The cultural activities each of the invaders brought with them. For example, Roman amphitheatres and Anglo-Saxon and Viking sagas.

## Chronology

Chronology forms a strong thread through AT 1 (see page 5).

## Diversity

The study of the social, cultural, religious and ethnic diversity of societies does not lend itself very easily to the invaders study unit and is perhaps best considered in later British core units. This is because of the lack of detailed evidence about the diversity in lifestyles among the Romans, Anglo-Saxons and Vikings. There would also be a risk of stereotyping the roles of women and men.

## Historical Sources

**Documents and printed sources** – A selection of documents appears in Chapter 7 and also in the pupil books. They are an exciting historical source putting the children into firsthand contact with the invaders. These documents have already been translated and can be further simplified so that they can be understood more easily. Often reading the original or putting it on tape will give the children the atmosphere and a paraphrase can then be used. Easier and more complex versions of the same document can be used with classes of widely differing abilities.

**Artefacts** – Original artefacts will be difficult to acquire and the schools' museum loan services are likely to be over-stretched. Copies are obtainable. Artefacts, like documents, bring the children into firsthand contact with the invaders.

**Pictures and photographs** – These can be a great stimulus for study and discussion and help to develop the skill of critical observation with the objective of learning, rather than just looking. It is most important that they are of genuine subjects as they are in *Collins Primary History* pupil books. Artist impressions should be avoided if at all possible unless they are used for comparison (AT1c), or evaluating evidence (AT3). Ideas for using the photographs in the pupil books can be found in Chapter 5. The photographs should be interrogated as evidence, for example: What does it show? What was it used for?

**Music** – This source is difficult with the Invaders because evidence is hard to find.

**Buildings and sites** – Not all archaeological sites have much to offer children of this age and some of the buildings can be hard to visualise unless there are reconstructions or models. Careful choice is essential and so is creating a list of the investigations that the children wish to carry out on arrival. Taking reference books can be a useful resource, together with cameras. Some investigations can be carried out by more than one group so that comparisons can be made during follow-up work. A list of the more well-known buildings and sites suitable for this age range can be found in Chapter 6.

**Computer-based material** – These might be used to make personal timelines, to use word processing and to work with maps on a concept keyboard. Data bases and graphs would be more difficult due to lack of evidence but could be used for itineraries, the length of Roman roads etc.

## Historical Enquiry and Communication
Pupils should have opportunities to;

- **Ask questions, choose sources for an investigation, collect and record information.** For example, how did the Romans supply all the needs of the soldiers stationed on and near Hadrian's Wall? Discuss the areas of research that might be useful - listing the soldiers' needs, visiting a Roman villa, considering Roman roads and water transport, letters found at Vindolanda etc.
- **Select and organise historical information.** For example, into categories such as, a soldier would need, a family would need.

Draw maps showing supply routes by land and sea. Use a database to consider distances and travelling time for soldiers and carts.

- **Present results orally, visually and in writing using a range of techniques.** For example, in a group do a display of the finds from the Sutton Hoo ship burial. Make models of some of the objects, label them as if in a museum and present the display to the class telling them what the discovery of the treasures tell us about Anglo-Saxon life.

## Links with the Cross-curricular themes

### Citizenship
- Consider the rights and wrongs of Boudica's rebellion. Were the rebels justified in fighting against Rome?

### Environmental Education
- Pupils can imagine their own environment as Roman, Anglo-Saxon or Viking children would have seen it. What has changed and is it an improvement?

### Health Education
- Comparison of modern hygiene standards with Roman times. Consider the baths, water supplies and drains in the Roman towns.

### Economic and Industrial understanding
- A Roman market could be set up using Roman coins designed and made by the pupils. This will raise awareness about coinage and how prices are set. Supply and demand may be more easily understood by younger pupils in terms of scarcity and plenty. After the Romans left, coins stopped coming into Britain, and bartering was used. The pupils could try this as a comparison to their Roman market.

# 2 Planning a History Study Unit

Detailed planning for the Invaders and Settlers HSU will vary depending on the age of the children. It may be the lead topic in a project on Neighbours or New and Old. Alternatively, it may form the starting point for a double unit, linking with a supplementary study unit such as ships and seafarers or land transport. Another alternative is a two-topic approach with 2 topics taught simultaneously with one being History-led and the other led by another subject, for example Invaders and Settlers with a Geography unit led by settlement.

Below is a checklist which teachers may find useful and reassuring as they are completing their planning for history.

**Checklist**

### 1 Familiarity with the PoS
a Which parts of the PoS will be concentrated upon and which will be treated with a "broad brush"?
b Is there any liaison with other Key Stages dealing with similar content, eg, Key Stage 3 - Roman Empire?
c How will we motivate the children initially? Which "ways in" shall we use?
d If there are aspects of the PoS where we need more knowledge/expertise, have we organised this? This Teacher's Guide will help.
e Are we combining this unit with another HSU?

### 2 Creating Units of Work
a Have we started with the Statements of Attainment (the skills) and devised investigative activities? (See the pupil books activities and chapter 5.)
b Have the General Requirements of the Report at Key Stage 2 been studied and consideration been given to them? (See chapter 1.)
c Have we built in differentiation so that we can challenge all the children and ensure effective learning?
d Have we designed some tasks which can be used for assessment and accepted that most of it will be "by outcome" rather than closed "by task"? (See chapter 3.)
e Do we have a policy for supporting National Curriculum History with additional resources?

### 3 Themes and Dimensions

Have we used this unit to support the National Curriculum cross-curricular themes and dimensions? Are any of them appropriate? See p8 of the Teacher's Guide.

*Collins Primary History* pupil books and Teacher's Guides will provide a sound basis for all the work required by the History statutory orders.

# Managing Time

It is quite possible that enough work has been generated by a HSU to occupy the class for a long time - rather than the length of time you can allow for it. What follows is one approach to this problem; there are many more.

1 Together you need to arrive at the "slim-line" plan. This involves looking at the range of activities and information you have got and dividing them between those opportunities which are crucial components, and those which are subsidiary.

2 Look at the crucial components. Consider differentiation and build in opportunities for assessment of a limited number of children each time. (See Chapter 3 of the Teacher's Guide)

3 Look at the subsidiary activities and choose some, if there is time, for all (or some of) the children to work on. This helps to build in differentiation and maintains pace. It also provides for individual interests.

## Evaluation of the unit - during and afterwards

It is important to be clear about what is being evaluated. It could be

a The teacher's original plan.

b The adaptations that the pupils' learning and choices have made to that plan.

c Whether enough time is/was spent on the unit.

d Whether the work is motivating/has motivated the children.

e Whether enough assessment has been carried out.

f Whether enough cross-curricular work has been carried out.

g Whether the pupils have developed an understanding of the content of the unit.

h Whether the pupils have enhanced their skills as historians - in particular those specified in the statements of attainment.

i Whether progression is being/has been achieved.

There are many more criteria for evaluation. It is best if teachers create their own additional lists.

# 3

# Assessment

For statutory purposes pupils must be assessed against the History Attainment Targets at, or near the end of, the key stage. For this a clear method of record-keeping needs to be established. Assessing every pupil activity or response is not really practical, and a more sensible way to proceed is to focus on a particular task for assessment purposes. There are many activities in the pupil books and in chapter 5 which could provide the basis for this. There are, however, additional tasks which have been included at the end of this chapter which provide some guidance on how judgement of levels might be made. Teachers might use them as examples on which to base alternative tasks.

This chapter aims to highlight some of the general issues associated with the assessment of history.

* SEAC recommends that children are told which skills the teacher is looking for in any task. An explanation of the attainment target required will give them a better opportunity to demonstrate their understanding and to take responsibility for their own learning.

* The assessment of the History ATs must be carried out when the pupil is engaged in historical enquiry or communication.

* Children's understanding and grasp of historical skills and concepts will grow gradually and need continued reinforcement. It is vital to build in the assessment tasks so that they appear as a natural part of the children's learning - rather than as a task tacked on to the end of the work.

* Introduce differentiated tasks which have a common starting point but which will soon present choices for the children. They can either take the simplest route or a more difficult route, perhaps involving more demanding reading or a keener understanding of concepts. Alternatively have the children split into ability groups and the same task given to each one but with different levels of teacher input depending on abilities.

* A set of questions and activities with specific outcomes can probably be most useful as a confirmation that a pupil or group of pupils have mastered certain skills or knowledge.

* The History ATs can be achieved orally. This can provide opportunities for the articulate and thoughtful child who finds written work hard.

* A limited number of children can be assessed on each occasion. It is important to remember that, to cover the 9 HSUs, at least 2

units will be covered in each year. This provides two opportunities in each year for the History SoAs to be assessed.

## Collecting the evidence of attainment

Collect evidence of the pupil's attainment in a variety of ways:

- Observing pupils at work, individually or in a group.
- Questioning, talking and listening to pupils.
- Considering materials produced by pupils and discussing these with them.

School records will have to:

- Show the pupil's performance in the history ATs.
- Show which aspects of the subject have been covered.
- Identify performance in cross-curricular elements.
- Establish the pupil's needs as a basis for further planning and teaching.

Oral assessment will form the basis of assessing a pupil's performance and teachers must discuss their interpretation of open-ended questions to ensure consistency.

Not every child in the class will need a detailed assessment on every AT while studying each PoS. A quick reference system to note progress will be useful. Each school will probably develop their own methods but one solution is to keep brief teacher records which can be amended:

A = attained it.
G = grasping the concept.
E = experienced the idea, but has not shown any understanding yet.

These letters could be noted in the teacher's records and dated. They can form a focus for discussion with the child or parents. AGE, or something similar, can be used throughout the school and supported by more detailed comments. For the teacher taking over a class it ensures that progression continues.

# Ideas for assessment activities

The activities are intended to be assessment focused and are set with this purpose in mind. The teacher will have to decide upon the appropriate questions and decide on the levels from the responses given, perhaps using the guidance given here.

## AT1c

Ask the children to conduct a comparison of the life of an invader with everyday life in modern Britain. Ask them to put their results in a table. Specific areas can also be chosen for the comparison, for example, country life, towns, burial etc.

| Possible results | Levels |
| --- | --- |
| The work communicates some important differences. | level 2 |
| Once they have achieved level 2, ask them to extend the comparison to another historical period eg Egyptian or Victorian times. | level 3 |

Talk to the children about the different aspects of the life of the invader they have learnt about. Ask them to present a display on their invaders and to talk about their work.

| | Levels |
| --- | --- |
| The work and discussion show an understanding of the different aspects. | level 4 |
| Discussion shows an understanding of the relationship between the different aspects. | level 5 |

## AT2

This activity is based on primary resource material about Vikings. The children need to read both pieces of written evidence on page 12 of the pupil book. Explain any difficult words and discuss the passages with the children. Encourage the children to compare the two pieces of evidence and evaluate them, using questions which will highlight the extent of the children's understanding of the different levels.

| Possible responses | Levels |
| --- | --- |
| A recognition that the two stories give different versions of what happened. | level 2 |
| An ability to distinguish between factual writing and a point of view. | level 3 |

A recognition that we do not always have enough evidence to be sure about what exactly happened. For example, we don't have the Viking side of the story.

level 4

This is best assessed when the children have nearly completed their work on the Vikings and their way of life. The Vikings have traditionally been portrayed as violent fighters. Discuss the fairness of this image in the light of the children's study of Viking settlement, trade, town life and jewellery.

level 5

## AT3

This activity focuses on the chapter about Sutton Hoo (pupil book pages 33-35). Discuss the discovery and ask the children to draw objects, copying them carefully. Talk about the treasures and what we can learn from them.

| Possible responses | Levels |
|---|---|
| The child can talk about the piece they are drawing. | level 1 |
| A recognition that the object might help them learn something about the person who was buried. | level 2 |
| The child can say what they can learn from the objects. For example, he was rich, he was a soldier etc. | level 3 |
| The child can talk about what the different objects, together with the writing of Bede, tell us. For example, the man was probably King Raedwald, he was probably a Christian etc. | level 4 |
| The child can comment on the usefulness and limitations of the Sutton Hoo treasures as evidence. | level 5 |

# Cross-curricular Links

A History-led major topic based on one of the HSUs can provide many cross-curricular opportunities. However, the History PoS are comparatively difficult to incorporate into another subject-led topic such as Science or Geography.

Below are ideas for an initial brainstorm on cross-curricular links.

## GEOGRAPHY

Map work eg: Invasion and settlement

Boudica's route

Planning and positioning of Roman roads and towns

Extent of Roman Empire

Local produce and development of trade

## ENGLISH

Recording and researching

Creative writing eg: Boudica's Rebellion p10 R, p5 ASV. Viking raids, p12-14 ASV

Different purposes of writing eg: diaries, chronicles, letters

Discussion eg: slaves, different points of view

Literature eg: stories (p8 R, p62 of guide), fiction (see Resources)

Language derivation p28-29 ASV, p21 R

## RE

Gods and myths (p26 R, p28 ASV)

## DRAMA

Role play eg: Boudica (p10 R)

Invasion of a village (p12-14 ASV), Alfred and Danelaw negotiations (p15-16 ASV)

## The Invaders

## MATHEMATICS

Time Line: using large numbers

Roman numerals

Mosaics: tessellation p8 ASV, p13 R

## MUSIC

Storytelling with music

## ART

Jewellery and decoration (p27, 34 ASV)

Illuminated manuscripts (p30 ASV)

Mosaics (p8 ASV, p13 R)

Pottery and clay

Drawing, painting, modelling, collage eg: Roman villas, village scenes

## SCIENCE

Forces and movement eg: oars and sails

Levers eg: for movement of stones and construction

## TECHNOLOGY

Planning, designing and constructing models eg: Viking ships, jewellery, homes, weaving and looms, Roman writing tablets, Roman armour, Hadrian's wall

R after a page number indicates The Romans pupil book. ASV after a page number indicates The Anglo-Saxons and Vikings pupil book.

# Guide to the Pupil Books

There are 2 pupil books for the Invaders and Settlers study unit. The Statutory Order says that pupils should have an overview of the three invasions and should study in depth one of the three invasions and settlements.

The Romans pupil book covers the Roman invasion in depth and also the essential information on the Anglo-Saxons and Vikings to provide a sense of chronology. The Anglo-Saxons and Vikings pupil book covers the essential information on the Romans but concentrates on the Anglo-Saxon and Viking invasions. The Anglo-Saxon and Viking invasions have been treated together. Unlike the Romans, the Anglo-Saxons did not leave Britain - the last kings in Britain before the Roman invasion of 1066 were in fact Anglo-Saxons, not Vikings. Therefore it is not possible to study either the Anglo-Saxons or Vikings in isolation.

This chapter has been divided into sections related to one or more chapters in the pupil books.

Each section headed by the pupil book chapter names and page numbers will contain;

a   Background historical information including additional evidence.

b   Guidance on the activities in the pupil books and their coverage of ATs.

c   Where appropriate, extra activities to provide extra choices from which teachers can create their own unit of work.

The activities in b and c aim to cater for a variety of levels within Key Stage 2, but obviously not all activities will be suitable for every class.

# The Romans

## The Invasions (pages 2-6)

### Historical information

At the time of Julius Caesar's brief invasions of Britain in 55 and 54 BC, Rome was about to complete her control over the area around the Mediterranean. When General Plautius invaded Britain in AD 43, the Roman Empire was reaching its greatest extent and was enjoying a period of relative peace with economic and cultural development.

There were two groups of people living in Britain. One were the Britons who were Iron Age farmers and miners of lead, gold and silver. They had created hill forts like Maiden Castle in Dorset and their ancestors had built Stonehenge but there is no record of a written language. They shared a common culture and spoken language with the second group of people - the Celts, who occupied much of Europe.

The Celts began arriving in Britain in about 100BC from northern France - and then more rapidly as Julius Caesar conquered Gaul. They settled in South East Britain and traded with the Romans in Gaul in corn, skins, cattle, hunting dogs and slaves.

Most of the written evidence we have of Britain at this time comes from the diary of Julius Caesar (104-44BC). These records were intended for the Senators in Rome to further his own political career.

Ceasar writes of the first invasion in 55BC;

> The man who carried the eagle of the tenth legion prayed to the gods and cried out, "Come on Lads! Jump if you don't want to lose your eagle to the enemy." He then leapt into the water and began wading towards the shore. The others followed, shouting that they must not shame themselves by losing their eagle.

The first invasion only lasted a few weeks before the 12,000 strong Roman army was forced to leave. The next year in 54BC, 32,000 men including 2,000 cavalry, invaded in 300 ships. Some of the ships were galleys rowed by slaves, others were trading vessels. Caesar landed in North Kent, crossed the Thames east of London, and allied with the Trinovantes tribe from the Essex area who were jealous of the Celtic king, Cassivellaunus.

In the third successful invasion, the Romans were helped by King Verica of the Atrebates tribe. The Roman Army, led by General Plautius, won the battle against the Celts without difficulty. Emperor

Claudius arrived with his court and some elephants for the triumphal entry into Colchester. He left after three weeks leaving instructions for the conquest of Britain.

The conquest of lowland Britain - as far west and north as the Fosse Way, running from Lincoln down to Exeter - was virtually complete by AD 59. The Romans set up forts along the Fosse Way and had obtained their prime objective - control over the rich farmland.

According to Roman sources, the Druids were an elite group of priests receiving seven years of oral training. They controlled the law and education. They were drawn from Britain and Europe and they demanded loyalty and obedience to the goddess Andrasta, the unconquerable. They produced dreadful punishments and death for the disobedient. Like the Christians later, they represented a genuine threat to Rome since they demanded obedience from their followers.

## Pupil book activities (page 6)

| Activity number | AT(s) covered | Comments |
| --- | --- | --- |
| 1 | AT2 | Caesar had plenty to gain by exaggerating the strength of his enemies. It made him look more successful. |
| 2 | AT3 | Develop as a co-operative activity in P.E. with children having made rectangular Roman shields. Let some children be the Roman "tortoise" and the rest be Celts high on the apparatus throwing down soft balls. |
| 3 | AT1b | After the ordering has been completed let a group further discuss the causes and consequences. For lower levels, discuss why the Celts were not ready to fight the Romans in AD43. For higher levels, consider reasons why the Celts did not win and what the consequences of the Celtic defeat were for King Verika. |
| 4 | AT1b | The crops and the silver, gold and tin from the mines were very badly needed by a large empire. |
| 5 | AT1b | The Druids would not accept Roman authority. |
| 6 | AT1a | |

## Other activities

1 How can we be sure the Romans ever came to Britain? Where can we find evidence? AT3

Above ground
* Words and language, eg place names, etc.

* Ruins, eg, Hadrian's Wall.

\*     Carvings and sculpture, eg, milestones.

\*     Writing, eg, Roman historians, Vindolanda letters.

Underground

\*     Archaeology, eg, Roman villas, forts and towns.

Use large sheets of paper and make sets from the groupings above. As the children go through the pupil books, let them add the evidence as it is discovered to the correct set. You may want to separate each Invader or treat it as an evidence activity without sub-sets.

2   Make a model using wet sand of Maiden Castle using the photo on page 5 as a reference. How easy would it be to defend? AT3

# Queen Boudica (Pages 7-10)

## Historical information

King Prasutagus of the Iceni tribe had made a treaty with the Romans and had become a client state. It seems that he thought he could best ensure the security of the Iceni by seeking to continue this relationship in his will. However, this relationship was an awkward anomaly and Rome were unlikely to want to continue it.

The seizure of all the Iceni property and possessions by the Romans was the catalyst for the revolt. Resentment against the Romans had built up, especially near Colchester, because of land which had been taken away from the Celts to give to the Roman army. In the Empire it was the custom to reward soldiers with farmland on their retirement after the normal 25 years service.

The exact site of the battle between Boudica's army and the Romans is not known. Paulinus had approximately 13,000 well trained troops to Boudica's 100,000 Celts. After the battle, Paulinus decided on revenge and was so cruel that the Romans asked for his re-call from Britain. It seems likely that there was famine as farming had been disrupted. The Romans went on to capture Anglesey and there were no more rebellions.

Our source for the story of Boudica, Tacitus, was a Roman historian whose father-in-law Agricola, was on Paulinus' staff in AD60. Later Agricola became Governor of Britain. Tacitus is considered reliable about factual matters but he had no tradition of objectivity. His history of the Roman Empire was called the Annals - only parts of it survive.

For extracts from Tacitus' annals see page 56.

## Pupil book activities (page 10)

| Activity number | AT(s) covered | Comments |
|---|---|---|
| 1 | AT2 | Ask questions. Why was there no account from Boudica's side? Would it have been the same? Can the children write part of the story from the Celtic viewpoint? |
| 2 | AT3 | See page 54. |
| 3 | AT1b | |
| 4 | AT3 | The burning of London appears as a horizontal line of ash in archaeological digs in London at the appropriate Roman level. |

| Activity number | AT(s) covered | Comments |
|---|---|---|
| 5 | AT1 AT3 | Acting out Boudica's revolt in small groups could form the central theme for learning about the Romans. Let the children think of themselves as part of Boudica's army. |

a) What would Boudica's army pass along the route (eg villas etc)? AT1a
b) What would they find once they entered the three Roman cities (eg life in Roman Towns)? AT1a
c) What kind of people came to join Boudica and who stayed away? AT1b
d) What were the roads like? AT3
e) Why were there no revolts after this one? AT1b

## Other activities

1 Stop the story after the Romans had ill-treated Boudica and her daughters. Let the class conduct a discussion as Boudica's advisers. What do they think she should do? Was the ill-treatment sufficient cause for rebellion? What might the consequences be? Record the suggestions. AT1b.

# Building Hadrian's Wall (page 11)

## Historical information

Agricola was governor in Britain and so his son-in-law, Tacitus, later had a firsthand source. Agricola probably had orders from Vespasian to conquer the whole island and so the Romans moved into Scotland. Later they built a turf wall, the Antonine Wall, between what we now know as Edinburgh and Glasgow but it was abandoned by about AD 160 because the lines of communication were too long and ambushes too frequent.

Hadrian's Wall was first built partly of turf and only over time reinforced with stone. It took about four years to build, beginning in AD122 and occupied 10 -15,000 men. It appears to have been manned largely by "auxiliary" soldiers recruited from the German area of northern Europe.

## Other activities

1 Older children might research Hadrian's Wall and the Great Wall of China and compare the two. AT1c.

2 Compare the photograph of Hadrian's wall with the aerial photograph of Maiden Castle. Which tells you more? AT3

# Living in a Country Villa: Farming (pages 12-15)

## Historical information

The rich farmland in lowland Britain was one of the Romans' reasons for invading and then conquering Britain. As they needed a constant supply of food for their armies and the cities throughout the Empire, they turned the small Celtic farms over to large-scale production. These large country villas provided food for the markets in nearby towns. They also sometimes acted as a centre for collecting taxes and repairing roads.

## Pupil book activities (pages 13,15)

| Activity number | AT(s) covered | Comments |
|---|---|---|
| (page 13) | | |
| 1 | AT1a | Make 2 collages, one for a Roman room and one for a modern room and compare. Make lists - <br>• These things are the same. <br>• These things are similar. <br>• Only the Romans had ... <br>• Only we have ... |
| 2 | | A design and technology activity. Let the children choose their own materials and designs. |
| 3 | AT1a | A comparison activity. |
| (Page 15) | | |
| 1 | AT3 | A study of different kinds of evidence. |
| 2 | AT1a | |
| 3 | | Encourage children to do their own research on Roman food. AT3 |
| 4 | | Potatoes were brought in from America in the 16th century. |

## Towns and Trade (pages 16-19)

### Historical information

Many of Agricola's towns were sited at the meeting places of the different tribes. A uniform grid divided the town itself into regular blocks. The public buildings were centred at the heart of the town. They were large and imposing, sometimes as high as 22 metres. The buildings were made of stone and bricks. Bricks were stamped to show the maker and were often faced with stone on important buildings.

### Pupil book activities (page 19)

| Activity number | AT(s) covered | Comment |
|---|---|---|
| 1 | AT1c | |
| 2 | AT3 | Roman taxes in Britain were paid in money or sometimes services or goods, particularly corn. Compare what the Romans did with their taxes to what we do with our taxes. AT1c. This activity also covers cross-curricular themes (citizenship, economic and industrial awareness). |
| 3 | AT1c | A comparison activity. |
| 4 | AT3 | Encourages detailed observation of sources. |

### Other activities

1  Look at the three carvings on page 17. Talk about the 3 different kinds of shop (permanent, use of trestles, foldaway shop). Design and make any one of these stalls. AT3

2  Can the children find the steelyard in the Butcher's shop and make one. See page 57.

# Slaves: Education (pages 20-21)

## Historical information

Slaves might be prisoners of war, convicted criminals, people unable to pay taxes or the children of slaves. For some, life could be hard and spent road building. However, some were very well educated and became bailiffs or foremen for their masters. At Roman forts some of the administration and letter writing was done by scribes who were slaves. There does not seem to have been too much of a stigma as it was possible for a freed slave to become a town councillor. Their achievements appear on grave stones.

## Pupil book activities (page 20)

| Activity number | AT(s) covered | Comments |
| --- | --- | --- |
| 1 | AT1a | A discussion activity which highlights changes in attitudes. |
| 2 | AT1b | Slaves were prisoners of war, convicted criminals, people unable to pay taxes or children of slaves. |

## Other activities

1 Let the children make wax tablets by melting wax or using plasticine on shallow trays and writing on the set wax with a sharpened piece of wood.

# Roman Transport (pages 22-23)

## Historical information

Until the Romans arrived there had been no roads in Britain, just trackway. The Romans needed a good network of communications to keep control over Britain and to connect the main towns and forts. Nearly 10,000 kilometres of Roman roads have been identified. They were built by military engineers, as straight as possible and built using local materials.

The document on page 22 of the pupil book telling us how the roads were made was written by a poet named Statius who wrote in the 1st century AD. Writing at the same time was Sicculus Flaccus;

> There are local roads which branch off state roads...These are maintained by the headmen in the counties...who normally charged the work to the landowners. Sometimes they gave to each landowner certain sections across his own land, which are kept up at his expense. At the end of the sections they put up notices to show which landlord has to keep up which sections over whose land.

Peutinger's medieval copy of a Roman road map of all the major roads of the Empire indicates that maps existed in Roman times. The most usual way to plan a journey, however, was to use itineraries - lists of places with mileage between. Also used were milestones. A Roman mile was 1,480 metres. Waterways were used as far as possible as a means of transport in Roman Britain, particularly for bulky and heavy loads. The Romans built Car Dyke which ran from Lincoln, south round the Wash. This was probably used for moving corn and other supplies northwards.

## Pupil book activities (page 23)

| Activity number | AT(s) covered | Comments |
|---|---|---|
| 1 | | A simple reference task for younger children. For older children, consider what supplies would be needed on Hadrian's wall. Page 24 of the pupil book could act as reference. |
| 2 | AT1b | It was often quicker than road transport. |
| 3 | AT3 | An opportunity to improve observational skills and to talk about the value of different types of evidence. |

## Other activities

1 Compare the document on road building in the pupil book with the document on this page. Which one tells you more about the Romans and in what way? AT3.

# A Roman Fort (pages 24-25)

## Historical information

Archaeologists believe that the fort at Vindolanda was occupied from around AD 90. Major army camps were quite large centres and had walls, baths, water supplies, granaries, temples, drilling grounds, administrative blocks, kitchens and stables. Although soldiers were not allowed to marry until they retired after 25 years of service there is evidence of family life at Vindolanda.

## Pupil book activities (page 25)

| Activity number | AT(s) covered | Comments |
|---|---|---|
| 1 | | Let the children work out a list of things which would be available in Roman times. |
| 2 | AT1b | A very open question which will let the children show what they understand. Tell the children that you want them to think about why the invitation was sent and move onto what it can tell us about conditions in the north at that time. |
| 3 | AT1c | |
| 4 | AT1c | The children could present their ideas in sets. |

# Gods and Goddesses: Daring to be a Christian (pages 26-27)

## Historical information

Roman Emperors found gods a convenient way of bolstering their government and sometimes tried to increase their power by declaring themselves to be gods. A temple dedicated to the deified Emperor Claudius was being built at Colchester at the time of Boudica's attack in AD60.

There were no problems in the area of religion if the conquered tribes accepted Roman gods and goddesses and combined their own with the Roman versions. Priests or leaders who demanded a different allegiance, such as the Druids in Britain or the early Christians in the Mediterranean, ran into trouble with the Romans.

Additional evidence of Christianity in Britain is limited and includes an inscription on a bowl found in Manchester which dates from around AD175 and the Mildenhall treasure, made in around AD350, which was found in Suffolk. This treasure contains silver vessels with Christian inscriptions and also some pagan ones.

The mosaic on page 29 shows the Greek letters X (Chi) and P (Pho). You can see these letters in the mosaic.

## Pupil book activities (page 27)

| Activity number | AT(s) covered | Comments |
|---|---|---|
| 1 | AT1b | A research and discussion activity. |
| 2 | AT1b | Christians would not now be prosecuted. |

## Other activities

1  Christians had to write in code during the Roman period. The following word square in Latin was carved on a wall in Cirencester and was a Christian code.

R O T A S
O P E R A
T E N E T
A R E P O
S A T O R

This meant, Arepo the sower carefully holds the wheels.

If you write the Latin words for Our Father twice like this:

```
                      P
                      A
                      T
                      E
                      R
      P A T E R N O S T E R
                      O
                      S
                      T
                      E
                      R
```

and cross off each letter in the word square which is the same, you are left with 2 A's and 2 O's. These stand for Alpha and Omega - 2 Greek words meaning the Beginning and the End. Jesus said he was the Alpha and Omega and so these letters had special meaning for the Christians.

2 Look at the photo on page 26 of objects in a child's grave from about just after the Roman invasion in AD 43. Pagans were buried with treasures which might be useful in the next life. What would the children have chosen to be buried with if they had lived in this period? AT3.

# How Long did the Romans Stay?: Thinking Back (pages 28-30)

## Historical information

The departure of the legions arose because of the difficulties in the Roman Empire. These included civil war and attacks from tribes living outside the Empire who took the opportunity to raid and invade. There was a gradual movement of people from Eastern Europe towards the west which, in time, created a shortage of land in Western Europe and helped to lead to the Anglo-Saxon invasions of Britain.

## Pupil book activities (pages 29-30)

| Activity number | AT(s) covered | Comments |
|---|---|---|
| (page 29) | | |
| 1 | AT3 | Children should show awareness that artefacts as evidence can help reconstruct a view of the past. |
| 2 | AT1b | Consider Boudica's revolt when the Celts were allowed to carry weapons. What was the consequence of the Celts not having weapons? What would be the different points of view on this point between the Romans and the Celts? AT2 |
| 3 | AT1a | |
| 4 | AT1b | Each of these 2 lists can be done by more than one group. Discussions and presentations to the rest of the class should follow using evidence to support their points of view. As this is a very open-ended activity it may be useful to note down any comments from the children which seem significant so that they can be checked against the ATs. Follow up discussions could confirm achievement. This could lead into activity 1 on page 30. |
| 5 | AT1b | What would the children have done after the Romans left with laws, defence etc? |
| (page 30) | | |
| 1/2 | AT3 | The activities are for children who have spent some time studying the Romans and are about to complete their work on the Invaders and Settlers with a brief look at the Anglo-Saxons and Vikings. |

## Other activities

1  How do the children react to the cartoon on page 29 as a source of evidence? Do they think the clothes are accurate? AT2

# After the Romans: the Anglo-Saxons and Vikings (pages 31-39)

## Historical information

This section in the pupil's book is a brief introduction to the Anglo-Saxon and Viking invasions and settlements. Please refer to the appropriate sections in this chapter on pages 34-50 for more detailed historical information on the Anglo-Saxons and Vikings.

## Pupil book activities (pages 32-39)

| Activity number | AT(s) covered | Comments |
|---|---|---|
| (page 32) | | |
| 1 | AT2 | Encourage the children to read as many of the legends of King Arthur as possible and to compare them. Try and find out when the legends were first recorded and compare on a time line. |
| 2 | AT3 | |
| (Page 34) | | |
| 1 | | Encourages research skills. Brighter children could compare evidence about St Patrick with that of Arthur or St Augustine. Why does the reliability and amount of the evidence vary? |
| 2 | AT1b | |
| 3 | | Cross-curricular links with RE. |
| (page 35) | | |
| 1 | | This lends itself to the cross-curricular theme of citizenship. The children could make their own rules for the classroom. Consider a trial period for the rules, and then an opportunity to evaluate and then to either change or continue with them. Do rules need sanctions in order to work? Which sanctions work best? |
| 2 | | Children could start a pupil's version of a school log-book which becomes the responsibility of a particular year group. What type of events would be recorded? In a few years it would be a useful resource for evidence and/or local history. |
| (page 38) | | |
| 1 | AT1a | Helps with sequencing skills. |
| 2 | AT2 | A good activity to see if children understand about different points of view. |

| Activity number | AT(s) covered | Comments |
|---|---|---|
| (page 39) | | |
| 1 | AT3 | What other types of evidence would the children expect to find? |
| 2 | AT1b | |
| 3 | | Can be done with individual pupils or groups. |

## Other activities

1 Either during the HSU or at the end, the children can make a time line for the invaders, from 55 BC to AD l065. The time line on page 53 will act as a basis. This activity could act as a focus for the work on this HSU. The level of detail will clearly depend on the age of the children. Let the children design their own class time line so making it also a design and technology activity. ATla

Encourage the children to ask questions:

a) how will they mark off time? In centuries?
b) which important events should be included and where?
c) how can we show that some invaders came and stayed while others left?

2 This activity will give children the idea of levels in an archaeological dig but it is not intended to be an exact scientific reproduction of a dig. It is best done at the end of the HSU. AT1a, AT3

*You will need:* fishtank; 3 kinds of material eg sand, gravel, compost; carpet tile to represent ground surface; toy houses, trees etc; 3 sheets of sugar paper; plastic trowel; pastry brushes; 3 plastic bags; modern day objects eg biro, coins etc; "Anglo-Saxon/ Viking" objects eg piece of old leather, piece of wood with runes carved on it, wool from a fleece etc, Anglo-Saxon brooch; "Roman" objects eg replica Roman coin, tile, bone comb, piece of lead piping etc.

Bury each group of objects, oldest first in 3 separate layers in the fishtank. Add the carpet tile and the houses etc.

First discuss with the children their understanding of what an archaeologist does and why. Show them the fishtank and discuss the pretend nature of the "dig". Emphasise that great care and gentleness is needed when touching the layers. Children will have to make a class list of questions and investigations they want to carry out. Let the children do the digging and let them describe what they have dug up, and to try to identify it. When questions and discussion are finished, place the object on the appropriate layer of sugar paper. Deductions as to an appropriate date can be made and the object labelled as in a museum. A presentation to another class may be made of the archaeological "find".

3   Compare the figures on the bronze helmet on page 33 with the model of the Roman soldier on page 9. AT1a

4   Compare the reconstructed Viking boat on page 39 with the Roman corn barge on page 23. AT1a

5   Compare the decoration of the prow of the Viking boat on page 36 with the Roman Christian mosaic on page 27. AT1a

6   Look at the statue of King Alfred on page 35. Do you think it was put up while he was alive or many years later? Is the statue like any of the other carvings in this book? There is some evidence in this book of what archaeologists think Anglo-Saxons wore. Do the clothes on this statue of Alfred look like Anglo-Saxon clothes? AT3

# The Anglo-Saxons and Vikings

## The Romans (pages 2-8)

### Historical information

This section in the pupil book is a brief introduction to the Romans in Britain which covers the essential information in the Programmes of Study. Please refer to the appropriate sections in this chapter, on pages 17-30, for more detailed historical information on the Romans.

### Pupil book activities (page 3)

| Activity number | AT(s) covered | Comments |
|---|---|---|
| 1 | AT1b | Encourage the children to decide on criteria eg. Things which helped Caesar, things which helped the Celts, why Plautius won, why the Celts lost. |
| 2 | AT2 | An introduction to the idea that the history we know is dependent on evidence that is left. |
| 3 | AT3 | What do they think each piece of equipment was for (page 2)? Can they learn anything about how the army fought (page 3)? |

### Other activities

1 Do the children understand what 'invasion' means? Start to compile a class glossary.

*Also see pages 18-19 for other activities.*

### Pupil book activities (page 5)

| Activity number | AT(s) covered | Comments |
|---|---|---|
| 1 | AT2 AT3 | There is a more detailed version of the story on page 56. |
| 2 | AT2 | Is rebellion ever right? Would the children think she was right if she had won? Is that a good way to decide? |

## Other activities

See pages 20-31 of this book.

## Pupil book activities (page 8)

| Activity number | AT(s) covered | Comment |
|---|---|---|
| 1 | AT3 | Help the children to choose a variety of sources. |
| 2 | AT3 | Ask the children to work out their process. This is a technology activity. |

## Other activities

1 With the children, invite parents or another class into the classrooom. The children's task is to plan how they will prove to their visitors that the Romans did come to Britain and then to present their proof. The visitors should be encouraged to ask questions. AT3

# What Happened Next?: Invitation or Invasion? (pages 9-11)

## Historical information

The Romans had left by AD 412 and the period which followed is sometimes called the Dark Ages. This is because there is so little reliable evidence and our knowledge of the period is therefore very limited. It is based on archaeological finds and some written evidence.

The major archaeological evidence comes from West Stow and Sutton Hoo in Suffolk for the Anglo-Saxons and Jorvik (York) for the Vikings.

Probably the most reliable Anglo-Saxon writer is the Venerable Bede who was a monk living in Northumbria who wrote in about AD 731. He drew on sources which are discussed in an activity for older children (page 37, activity 3). The children can read part of his account of the coming of the Anglo-Saxons on page 10 of the pupil book and a fuller version is to be found on page 58. The Anglo-Saxon Chronicles also provide some of the best written source material. They were organised by King Alfred of Wessex in around AD 860.

The struggle between the Celts and the Anglo-Saxons continued sporadically for about 120 years and it is this period which has always been associated with King Arthur. Legend has suggested that he led the Celts against the Invaders. Recently this has been reinforced by scholars deciphering the calendars of monks. The following comments have been found about Arthur on the calendars:

> AD 518. The battle of Badon in which Arthur and the Britons were victorious.

> AD 539. The strife of Camlann in which Arthur and Modred perished and there was plague in Britain.

By about AD 577 the Anglo-Saxons had fought their way to control lowland Britain (this had taken the Romans rather less than 20 years). They had set themselves up in a series of small kingdoms the boundaries of which altered depending on the strengths, alliances and ambitions of the leaders.

## Pupil book activities (page 11)

| Activity number | AT(s) covered | Comments |
| --- | --- | --- |
| 1 | AT3 | Archaeologists would find no remains showing signs of life from this period. There might be signs of ruined buildings. This might be a good time to introduce Fishtank Archaeology (see pages 32-33). |

| Activity number | AT(s) covered | Comments |
|---|---|---|
| 2 | AT1b | Can an invitation turn into an invasion? You could role play birthday parties which have become a disaster because 'guests' become 'invaders'. |
| | AT2 | Let half the group define invitation and the other half invasion and compare their meanings. It may be that they have things in common. |
| 3 | AT1a AT2 | Add Bede and the invasions to the time line. Bede read old sources to find out about history. |

## Other activities

1   Examine the extract from Bede on page 10 of the pupil book. The children need to be told that this is a translation, that the language has been made easier for them and that the dots indicate parts of the story which have been left out.

Let the children decide what they want to find out from the document about the invasion. What questions will be useful?

Perhaps you will end up with a list of:
When? AT1 - chronology
Who? AT3 - use of evidence
Why? AT1b - cause and consequence
What? AT1b - cause and consequence
How? AT3 - use of evidence

Can the children work out whether Bede sympathised with one side or the other? (He disliked the invaders because at the time they were pagan and destructive). AT2

2   Do some work on the legends of King Arthur. Let the children consider the difference between legend and history. Does the evidence from the calendars make a difference? AT2, AT3

3   This activity is intended for older children but parts of it could well be used with younger children. Ask them to examine the accuracy of Bede's account of the Anglo-Saxon invasions with reference to his sources. You will need Bede's full account which is to be found on page 58 and the extracts from a variety of his sources on page 59. AT1, AT2, AT3

A: **Checking on how much evidence supports Bede about WHEN they came.**
   **Check 1:** Bede wrote that the Invaders came in AD 449 and some others shortly afterwards. How long afterwards was Bede writing? Is it important?

   **Check 2:** Bede obtained some of his information from Gildas but Gildas also wrote that Hadrian's Wall was built some time after AD 300. Look back to see if he was right. Is it important?

**Check 3:** Look at the date that Germanus visited Britain. Are raids the same as invasions?

**Check 4:** Look at the date mentioned in the French chronicle. Does this support Bede?

**Check 5:** Final check on when they came. How much of the evidence fits together?

**B: Check on how much evidence supports Bede about WHO came.**
**Check 1:** List the people Bede mentions and where they settled.

**Check 2:** Compare Procopius' people with those of Bede. Archaeologists have found villages in the Frisian area (see map on page 10 of the pupil book) which were deserted about AD 425-475. Can you draw any conclusions from this?

**Check 4:** Archaeologists have dug up burial grounds from this period in England. They found that people were buried with objects that were the same as those the invaders used in the lands Bede says they came from. Does this help?

**Check 5:** Final check on Who came? How much of the evidence fits together?

**C: Checking on how much evidence supports Bede on HOW they came.**
**Check 1:** Bede says they came in three boats. Very big rowing boats have been dug up by archaeologists from this time. Perhaps they had a sail and they held about 40 men. It would take several days to row across the sea.

Roughly how many men came with Hengist and Horsa?

**Check 2:** More boats came when Hengist and Horsa sent their message. If 2 boats came how many men would there be for the army? How many if there were 4 or 6 or 8 boats? Can you make a graph?

**Check 3:** Use the graph to compare with Bede's writing: 'It was not long before these people crowded into Britain...'

**Check 4:** Bede says that people 'began to live in terror'. Do the other sources support this?

**Final Check:** Make a final evaluation of Bede. How useful is his evidence in learning about the Invasions?

4   Use Bede's writing to tell the story in pictures (see page 58 for the fuller version). This could be developed to make a dramatic reconstruction with half the class as invaders and the rest as Britons. AT1a, AT2

5   On photocopiable page 61 Bede's evidence has been made into a story. How much of the story is fiction? Can they highlight the 'evidence' or the 'fiction'? AT2, AT3

# The Vikings (pages 12-14)

## Historical information

The chief motivation for Viking raids and invasions seems to have been an acute shortage of land and therefore food supply in their homelands in Norway, Sweden and Denmark, and a culture which was dedicated to valour and bravery. They were helped by the advanced design and technological superiority of their longships. These longships needed only about 74cms depth of water, could sail near to the wind, could carry about 70 men and were faster than any other ships. (For further information about Viking ships see page 49).

## Pupil book activities (page 14)

| Activity number | AT(s) covered | Comments |
|---|---|---|
| 1 | AT2 AT3 | We cannot be sure which was the first raid as there is not enough precise evidence. |
| 2 | AT2 | The monks and priests were normally the only people who were literate. The Vikings arrived in Britain as pagans. The monks would naturally be against the Vikings. |
| 3 | AT1a AT2 | The children will have to write from the Viking point of view. |
| 4 | AT3 | Comparing evidence. |

## Other activities

1   Look at the picture on page 13. How can you tell it is a modern reconstruction? (Bus, street lights, radio masts, TV aerial, modern ships.) AT3

2   Compare this map of the Viking invasions with the one on page 36.

3   Look at the sentences on page 60. **A** tells the story from the Viking point of view and **B** from the Anglo-Saxon point of view. Younger children can chronologically sequence a selection of the basic sentences from **A** or **B**. Then give one group of children the sentences from **A** and the other group the sentences from **B**. Ask them to tell or dramatise the story. Can they see any difference? AT1a, AT2

4   For other activities connected with Viking ships see page 50.

# King Alfred
# (pages 15-18)

## Historical information

This chapter gives a full picture of King Alfred who is an important figure in the history of the invasions. Alfred was a remarkable king, scholar, law maker and fighter. He lived from AD 849 until AD 899.

Alfred was the second son of the king of Wessex and spent much of his time fighting in the army of Wessex against the Vikings. The Anglo-Saxons made a number of alliances against the Vikings but were gradually out-manouvered and out-fought. By the time Alfred succeeded his brother in AD 871 he was carrying on the struggle with no effective help.

In 877 Alfred sent his troops home for Christmas. The Vikings attacked him by surprise and he had to escape into the marshlands. It is this flight through the Athelney marshes near Glastonbury which is normally associated with the story of Alfred and the cakes. However, the story is not mentioned by Alfred's friend and biographer, Asser. It first appears in the story about the life of a saint, rather than Alfred, some years after 1066. It is not until a 1904 biography of Alfred that he is associated with the cakes.

The Anglo-Saxon chronicles arose from Alfred's decision to call in all the records and calendars which had been kept by the monks in Latin. These were translated into the vernacular (Anglo-Saxon English) and about 9 copies were despatched to various monasteries to be continued by them. Together, the existing versions form one of the most important sources of evidence for this period in Western Europe.

The sword shown on page 15 was found at Abingdon. Alfred's Jewel on page 17 is thought to have been made for one of the bishops. It is made of gold and crystal and was used as a 'finger' to follow words when reading.

## Pupil book activities (page 18)

| Activity number | AT(s) covered | Comment |
|---|---|---|
| 1 | AT1a | Put Alfred and the Vikings on the time line. The Vikings arrived before Alfred was born. |
| 2 | AT1a AT2 | Discuss the criteria the children will use. Can they make two sets of reasons: Why was he great? Why was he good? |
| 3 | AT2 AT3 | A good way to show that selection of material determines what we know about the past and therefore our understanding of history. |

## Other activities

1  Tell or read to the children the story of Alfred and the cakes and ask them to check up at home whether it is true or not. Collect and sort the answers the children bring, focusing on the reliability of the evidence. Let them take a vote on whether the story is true. Then tell them about the writer in 1904 who borrowed a good story about someone else and wrote it about Alfred. Ask them why they think this was done and what their opinion of the writer is. What does this mean we have to do when we hear another History story? Do any of the children show an understanding of AT2 level 5, that popular accounts of the past may differ from what we know actually happened?

2  Use a magnifying glass to look at the decoration on the Anglo-Saxon sword and draw the patterns you see. Where else in the book can you find Anglo-Saxon decoration? Are the patterns the same?

# Living Together: Living in the Country (pages 19-23)

## Historical information

Although the Anglo-Saxons and Vikings appear very similar there were some differences.

a  They arrived over 300 years apart. The Vikings met a coherent political structure whereas the Anglo-Saxons encountered a more confused situation.

b  The Vikings seem to have been more interested in town life and trading overseas. The Anglo-Saxons were developing this side of life at about the time the Vikings arrived.

c  There is some archaeological evidence that the Anglo-Saxons found some deserted farms and in some cases settled with less opposition than the Vikings met.

d  The Viking long ships, and their slower trading vessels, were more sophisticated than those of the Anglo-Saxons. They saw Britain as only one of many destinations and they travelled much more widely.

More detailed information about the West Stow archaeological site and the reconstructions can be obtained from the address given on page 51. Otherwise there is little evidence about country life. The Anglo-Saxon village at West Stow existed at about the same time as the Sutton Hoo ship was buried. You may want to look at the two chapters together.

## Pupil book activities (pages 19, 23)

| Activity number | AT(s) covered | Comments |
|---|---|---|
| (page 19) | | |
| 1 | AT1b | Examining cause and consequence. |
| (page 23) | | |
| 1 | AT3 | The archaeologists would have found seeds, animal bones, the remains of houses etc. in the soil. |
| 2 | AT3 | Farming jobs, building, making clothes, fetching water, collecting firewood and herbs, household activities, making tools, plates etc. |
| 3 | AT1c | They had nearly everything they needed for daily life. The children could make a comparison with what people think they need now for everyday life. |
| 4 | AT3 | Wood rots away but the burned wood survives in the soil. This gave the archaeologists new evidence about the shape of the houses. |

| Activity number | AT(s) covered | Comments |
|---|---|---|
| 5 | AT3 | A technology activity involving close observation skills. It could be extended to make a whole model village. |

## Other activities

1 Write the following sentences on separate pieces of paper.

> They needed more land to farm for food.
> They wanted new houses.
> They wanted to raid and rob and then go away.
> Vortigern had promised them land.
> They came to fight the Picts and Scots.
> They thought it would be easy to stay.
> They wanted fame and glory.
> They wanted the gold, silver and tin from the mines.
> Britain was just one of several places to which they went.
> There was no room in the villages at home.
> Their boats were the fastest and the best.
> The Britons were cowardly.
> The land was fertile.

Let the children gradually sort the sentences into reasons why the Vikings invaded and reasons why the Anglo-Saxons invaded. They will probably find they need intersecting Venn diagrams. The sentences can be stuck on and the work displayed. AT1b, AT3

# Building Towns (pages 24-27)

## Historical information

The quality of the evidence about Jorvik arises from the damp ground in which the archaeological remains have lain. Jorvik was the leading city in the Danelaw from AD 866.

Most of the houses there were built by digging a cuboid out of the ground. The early houses seem to have had earthen floors. Wooden posts were hammered into the floor, spaced out round the walls. Strong twigs were woven in and out to make the walls. There may have been some daub placed in the walls. Later, planks of wood were used for the floor and also for the horizontal part of the wall, instead of twigs. There is no evidence about the roofs - possibly they were thatched. The houses were about 6.8m long and 4.4m wide and the roofs started about 50cms above the ground.

## Pupil book activities

| Activity number | AT(s) covered | Comments |
|---|---|---|
| 1 | AT1c | Identifying differences between times in the past. |
| 2 | AT3 | The making of coins was politically significant and a coiner could make a fortune if he were dishonest. |
| 3 | AT1c | Plastic had not been invented. |
| 4 | AT3 | Examining the nature of archaeological evidence. |
| 5 |  | Salt was used to preserve food. |

## Other activities

1  Look at the date of the helmet. Do you think it was a Viking helmet? (The helmet has been dated before the arrival of the Vikings). AT3. For further information and activities about helmets, see page 47.

## New Words (pages 28-29)

### Historical information

The Anglo-Saxons used runes but gradually began using the alphabet at the end of the eighth century AD. Both Anglo-Saxons and Vikings used runes for simple messages, rather than with any magical associations.

Archaeologists had thought that the places with Viking names were settlements created by them. Digging has revealed that many of them had been Saxon and had been renamed.

### Pupil book activities (page 29)

| Activity number | AT(s) covered | Comments |
|---|---|---|
| 1 | | The children could write messages the invaders might have written. |
| 2 | | Saturday was named after Saturn, the ancient god and the planet. Sunday is the day of the sun. |
| 3 | AT3 | Most of the Viking places will be found in the Danelaw and some in the Cumbria area. |
| 4 | AT3 | Using maps and place names as evidence. |

### Other activites

1 Use the description of Thor for artwork or creative writing. Can the children see similarities with some modern characters with supernatural powers, such as Superman? Do we enjoy the same kinds of stories as our ancestors? AT1a

## The Invaders Change: Bede (pages 30-32)

### Historical information

Bede (AD 673-735) went to the monastery of Monkwearmouth as a boy and then on to the monastery of Jarrow where he taught and wrote 36 different books. Although he used dubious sources such as Gildas, historians have found him generally accurate where they have other evidence to compare. The monasteries represented the flowering of scholarship in the midst of a period where evidence of society is scanty and war-like. It is the time when Iona and then Lindisfarne were centres of learning and holiness. The picture of Bede on page 32 is from the later 12th century AD.

### Pupil book activities (pages 31, 32)

| Activity number | AT(s) covered | Comments |
|---|---|---|
| (page 31) | | |
| 1 | | Let the children decide how they will find out the answer. |
| 2 | AT3 | The children can experiment with blocks, rollers and boats. The Anglo-Saxons used water transport as far as possible. |
| 3 | AT3 | Do the children know what a saint is? Can they decide what they want to find out before they begin? |
| (page 32) | | |
| 1 | AT2 AT3 | The children can draw on their research about Bede's version of the invasion. See pages 37-38. |
| 2 | AT1b,c | Comparing past and present and giving reasons for the development. |

### Other activites

1 Can the children collect all the references in the book to monks, monasteries and Bede and see what they have learned? AT3

2 Compare the church on page 31 with the outside of the church or chapel nearest to your school. What is the same and what is different? AT1c

# Sutton Hoo (pages 33-35)

## Historical information

The first thing to note is the chronology. The burial at Sutton Hoo is dated at about AD 625 and is thought to be that of King Raedwald of East Anglia, who was the high king at the time. Therefore the burial occurred during the time that the settlement at West Stow was inhabited. The two sites are only about 40 miles apart.

There was an astonishing array of treasure in this burial ship. When the archaeologists discovered the ship the marks left by the wood were clear to see, although the wood itself had disintegrated with age. Many of the rivets had remained in their original place. This gave the archaeologists a clear idea of the shape of the ship.

The winged dragon on page 34 of the pupil book is of gilt-bronze and was part of the decoration for a round shield. Other treasures found include a shoulder clasp of gold and garnets, silver bowls, a lyre and a ceremonial sceptre with a bronze stag on the top.

Archaeologists have found helmets because they were made of metal and have survived in the soil. The helmet on page 34 is a reconstruction of the original found at Sutton Hoo. The original can be seen on page 11. The Jorvik helmet, on page 27, is another Anglo-Saxon helmet and has knitted metal neck guards allowing for flexibility. Examples of Viking helmets can be seen on the models from the Jorvik museum.

## Pupil book activities (page 35)

| Activity number | AT(s) covered | Comments |
|---|---|---|
| 1 | AT1c AT3 | The children can also make comparisons with the Roman helmet on page 5. |
| 2 | AT3 | We know from the scientific dating of the various objects and the level of soil at which they were found. This is an ideal time to do some Fishtank Archaeology (see pages 32-33). |
| 3 | | Improves observational skills. |
| 4 | AT3 | Sometimes newly baptised Christians were given 2 spoons marked Saul and Paul, reflecting the conversion of Saul who changed his name to Paul when he became a Christian. The story can be found in Acts, chapters 9 and 13. |
| 5 | AT2 | Christian treasures were found but it was not a Christian burial. There is no right answer as there is not enough evidence to be sure. |

## Other activities

1   Read the story of Raedwald and Edwin on page 63. It is based on the writings of Bede. The story lends itself to drama, to a consideration of people's motives (AT1b), to sequencing (AT1a) and to a comparison of different types of evidence. Does the story help them understand the Anglo-Saxons more or less or the same as the treasures at Sutton Hoo or West Stow? AT3

2   Reading parts of Beowulf or other children's versions of the sagas will help the children understand more about the culture and values of the invaders.

3   This is a good opportunity to consider the artistic achievements of the Anglo-Saxons. The children can recreate some of the designs and patterns using a magnifying glass. AT3

## Vikings All Around: Thinking Back (pages 36-38)

### Historical information

The Vinland saga refers to a journey which began in about AD 985 when America was sighted after the hero, Eric, was blown off course in fog. It was not written down until the 12th and 13th centuries.

The picture on page 37 shows the Gokstad ship which was found in Norway. In 1893 a replica of the Gokstad ship was built and was sailed to America by Captain Magnus Andersen. He wrote, 'We often had the pleasure of darting through the water at speeds of 10 and even sometimes eleven knots. The finest merchant ships of our day have practically the same type of bottoms as Viking ships.' The Gokstad ship was 23.3m long and 5.25m wide in the middle. It needed about 92cms depth of water to sail in when fully loaded. The mast was probably about 10m long and the sail was made of white wool with red stripes sewn on.

Viking ships represented a great advance in ship building technology. Caesar had used galleys rowed by slaves as part of the Roman invasion fleet but they were not much good at sailing into the wind. The technology was not much advanced when the Anglo-Saxons invaded using a mixture of sailing boats which could also be rowed.

### Pupil book activities

| Activity number | AT(s) covered | Comments |
|---|---|---|
| (page 37) | | |
| 1 | AT3 | The children might list various things the Vikings could have left behind as evidence. In fact, runes were found in Constantinople and evidence of farms in Greenland and Iceland. Monks wrote about raids on the coast of Western Europe. |
| (page 38) | | |
| 1 | AT1b | Causes and consequences. Comparison of motives. |
| 2 | AT3 | Books, documents, words and place names, gravestones and burials, sites: Jorvik, West Stow, Sutton Hoo; reconstructed buildings, coins, jewellery, carvings, sagas, clothes, weapons, ships. |
| 3 | AT3 | Planning, presentation and evaluation of evidence. |
| 4 | AT3 | Consider all the different types of evidence in the answer to activity 2. |

## Other activities

1  Draw out the actual size of the Gokstad ship in the playground. How many people will fit in it? Remember to leave space for masts and oars. Can you make a scale model of a Viking ship, using the picture on page 37 and the reconstruction on page 13?

# 6 Resources

## Useful books for pupils

| | |
|---|---|
| History in Evidence: Roman Britain | *Wayland 1852105747* |
| History in Evidence: Saxon Britain | *Wayland 1852105755* |
| History in Evidence: Viking Britain | *Wayland 1852105771* |
| The Romans/Vikings: Fact and Fiction by R. Place | *Cambridge University Press 0521315727* |
| Eagle of the Ninth by R. Sutcliffe (Roman historical novel for older children) | *Puffin Books 0140308903* |
| The Sword in the Stone by T.H. White (Arthurian legends) | *Armada Lions 0006742009* |

## Useful books for teachers

| | |
|---|---|
| In search of the Dark Ages by M.Wood | *BBC Books 056336291X* |
| The Anglo-Saxon Chronicles by A. Savage | *Macmillan, London 0333488814* |
| Sutton Hoo ship burial | *British Museum Publications 0714105544* |
| History of the English Church and people by Bede | *Penguin Classics 0140440429* |
| Yorvik Viking Centre Information Pack | |
| Archaeology in the Primary School | *Council for British Archaeology* |

## Places to visit

**General**

London — British Museum

**Roman**

| | |
|---|---|
| Suffolk | - Ipswich Museum |
| Gloucestershire | - Corinium museum, Cirencester |
| | - Chedworth Roman villa |
| West Sussex | - Fishbourne Palace, Chichester |
| Kent | - Lullingstone villa |
| Avon | - Roman Baths Museum, Bath |
| Essex | - Colchester Museum |
| Cheshire | - Chester Museum |
| Northumberland | - Vindolanda Fort and Museum, Chesterholm |
| | - Housesteads Fort and Museum |
| Gwent | - Roman Legionary Museum, Caerleon |
| Glasgow | - Hunterian Museum |

**Anglo-Saxon**

| | |
|---|---|
| Suffolk | - Anglo-Saxon Village, West Stow, Bury St. Edmunds |
| Suffolk | - Sutton Hoo (site of excavation, treasures in British Museum) |

**Viking**

| | |
|---|---|
| Yorkshire | - Jorvik Viking Centre, Coppergate, York |
| Northumberland | - Priory Museum, Lindisfarne |

# Time Line

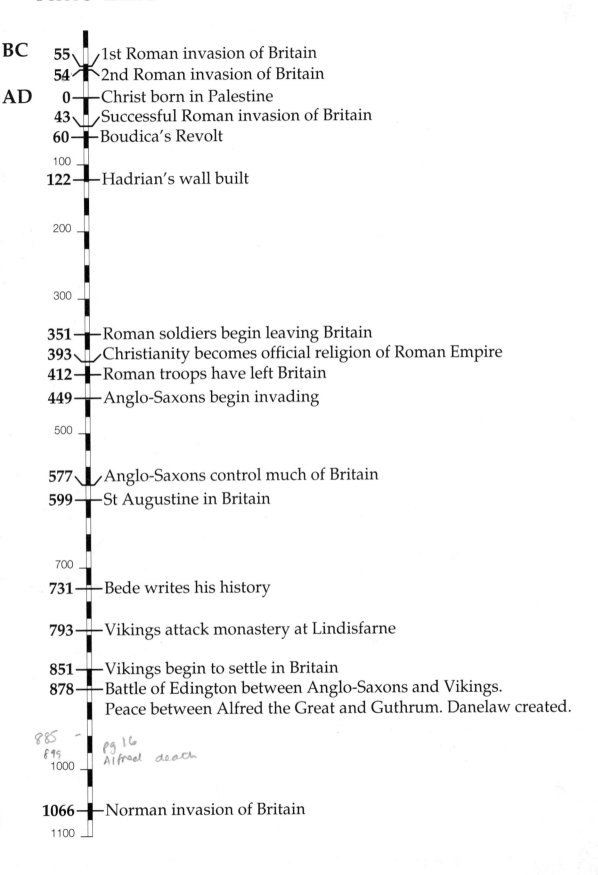

**BC**

**55** — 1st Roman invasion of Britain
**54** — 2nd Roman invasion of Britain

**AD**

**0** — Christ born in Palestine
**43** — Successful Roman invasion of Britain
**60** — Boudica's Revolt
100
**122** — Hadrian's wall built

200

300

**351** — Roman soldiers begin leaving Britain
**393** — Christianity becomes official religion of Roman Empire
**412** — Roman troops have left Britain
**449** — Anglo-Saxons begin invading
500

**577** — Anglo-Saxons control much of Britain
**599** — St Augustine in Britain

700
**731** — Bede writes his history

**793** — Vikings attack monastery at Lindisfarne

**851** — Vikings begin to settle in Britain
**878** — Battle of Edington between Anglo-Saxons and Vikings.
Peace between Alfred the Great and Guthrum. Danelaw created.

885 —
899     pg 16
1000    Alfred death

**1066** — Norman invasion of Britain
1100

# Roman Britain

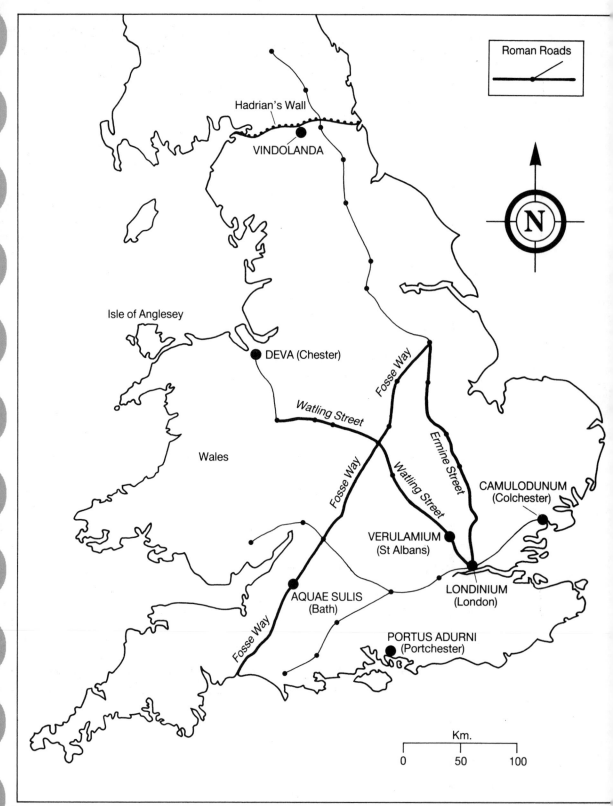

Roman Roads

Hadrian's Wall

VINDOLANDA

Isle of Anglesey

DEVA (Chester)

Fosse Way

Watling Street

Wales

Fosse Way

Ermine Street

Watling Street

CAMULODUNUM
(Colchester)

VERULAMIUM
(St Albans)

LONDINIUM
(London)

AQUAE SULIS
(Bath)

Fosse Way

PORTUS ADURNI
(Portchester)

N

Km.

0    50    100

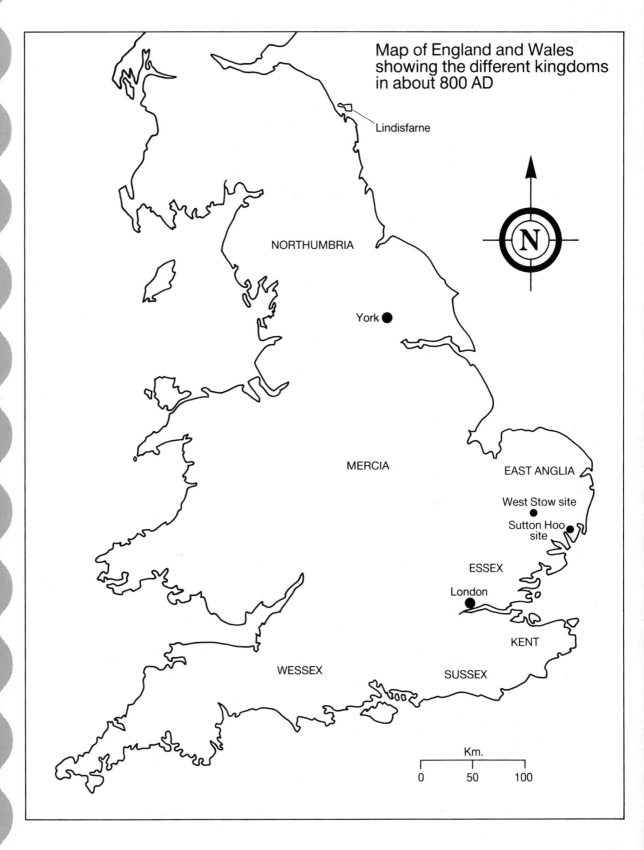

Map of England and Wales
showing the different kingdoms
in about 800 AD

Lindisfarne

N

NORTHUMBRIA

York ●

MERCIA

EAST ANGLIA

West Stow site
●

Sutton Hoo ●
site

ESSEX

London
●

KENT

WESSEX

SUSSEX

Km.

0      50      100

# Boudica

*Ideas for using this material can be found on page 20.*

*From Dio Cassius, a Roman historian*

She (Boudica) was very tall, and her appearance was terrifying, for her eyes flashed fiercely and her voice was harsh. A mass of red hair fell down to her hips, and around her neck was a twisted gold necklace; over a tunic of many colours, she wore a thick cloak fastened with a brooch...She clutched a spear ...

*From Tacitus' Annals*

### Boudica's attack on Colchester

Mad women went about raving and fore-telling doom... Hoping the Temple of Claudius would protect them and misled by secret rebel supporters of Boudica ... the Romans failed to build a rampart and ditch to defend themselves... Cerialis, commander of the 9th legion, was marching to the rescue when he was ... attacked and cut to pieces.

### Attack on London and St Albans

Paulinus ...decided to sacrifice that one city (London) in order to save the whole province. Neither tears ... nor appeals could sway him ... The same disaster happened in Verulamium (St Albans), for the barbarians ... headed for places where there were riches and where the defences were light.

### The battle

At this time, Paulinus having (about 10,000 men) prepared for ... battle. He chose a position in a narrow pass, protected to the rear by woods ... He drew up (his army) in close order ... The British forces ran riot all over the field in their mobs on horseback or on foot. They had never appeared in greater numbers and they were so confident that they had even brought along their wives to see their victory, putting them on wagons around the edge of the battlefield.

At first the legionaries stood their ground. Then, as soon as the attacking enemy came close enough ... they hurled their javelins and burst forward ... the cavalry rode down all (the enemy who still stood). The rest of the Britons turned and ran - but could not escape as they were trapped by the ring of wagons round the field. The Romans killed even the British women ... It was a glorious victory.

# Making a steelyard

Look at the picture of the butcher's shop on the bottom of page 17 in The Romans. Can you see the steelyard on the right which the butcher used to weigh the meat?

The butcher hung the meat on the hook and moved the weight along the steelyard arm until the arm was level. He then read the weight off by looking at the printed scale on the arm.

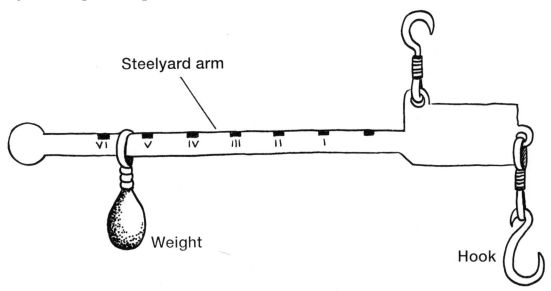

Steelyard arm

Weight

Hook

Try making your own steelyard.

**You will need**
ruler, string, felt-tip/biro to be a weight, something to weigh

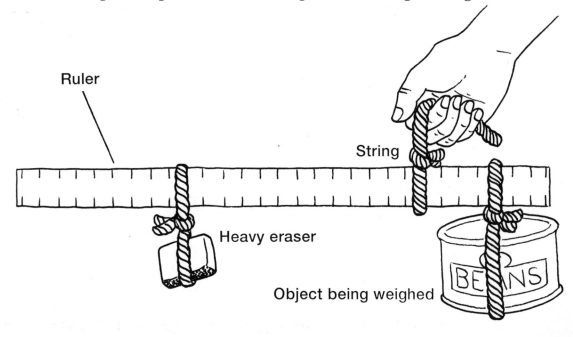

Ruler

String

Heavy eraser

Object being weighed

© 1992 Collins Educational

# The Arrival of the Anglo-Saxons

*Ideas for using this material can be found on pages 37-38*

*From Bede's Ecclesiastical History, written about AD 731.*

In the year of our Lord 449 the Angles or Saxons came to Britain at the invitation of King Vortigern in three longships and were granted lands in the eastern part of the island on condition that they protected the country: however their real intention was to rule it.

They, the Anglo-Saxons, engaged the enemy advancing from the north, defeated them and sent back messages to their homeland adding that the country was fertile and the Britons cowards.

So a larger fleet quickly came over with a great body of warriors and together they made an unbeatable army. They also received land to settle among the Britons. They were to defend the country in return for regular pay.

These men came from the three strongest tribes in Germany, the Saxons, the Angles and the Jutes. They settled in Kent, in the Isle of Wight and the land near it. They also settled in East Anglia, in Mercia and in Northumberland.

Their first chiefs were probably the brothers, Hengist and Horsa. It was not long before these people crowded into Britain and the Britons, who had invited them, began to live in terror.

... The Anglo-Saxons made an alliance with the Picts, and began to turn against the Britons. They wanted more food and threatened to take the whole land if they did not get it...

... These pagan conquerors devastated the cities and countryside... Buildings, priests and people were destroyed by fire and the sword and there was no-one left to bury the dead.

## Bede's sources

*Ideas for using this material can be found on pages 37-38*

**A** Gildas, a British monk living in Wales wrote about the conquest of Britain. He died about AD 572.

> The fierce Saxons were admitted to the island.

**B** Germanus, a monk from Gaul, visited Britain in AD 428 and found Britain:

> terrified by invaders.

**C** A French chronicle in AD 441 recorded:

> Britain ... was subjected to the domination of the Saxons.

**D** Procopius was a Roman writing after AD 500.

> The Angles, Saxons, and Frisians went to Britain.

# The Arrival of the Vikings

*Ideas for using this material can be found on page 39*

### The Viking Story

Three fast Viking ships arrived at the port.

The Vikings landed.

The Vikings set up a market stall.

Beaduheard, the Anglo-Saxon, galloped up with his men.

Beaduheard violently ordered the Vikings to follow him.

Beaduheard's men moved towards the Vikings.

There was a fight.

Beaduheard was killed.

### The Anglo-Saxon Story

Beaduheard was the servant of King Brihtric of Wessex.

Beaduheard heard that the Vikings had come.

Beaduheard and his men galloped to the port.

He thought the Vikings were merchants.

He ordered the Vikings to go with him.

He wanted to take them to the King.

He hoped the King would reward him.

The Vikings killed Beaduheard.

# The Story of Hengist and Horsa

*Ideas for using this material can be found on page 38*

### The Message

Hengist and Horsa sat quite still. The messenger stood in front of them and watched. King Vortigern, in England, had sent him across the sea to ask Hengist and Horsa for help against the Picts and Scots. Would they do what King Vortigern wanted? The brothers looked at each other and smiled, then Hengist winked at Horsa and Horsa winked back.

The messenger was given a good supper and a place to sleep in the straw near the fire. He had listened to a new saga and his head was full of the story he would tell when he got back to King Vortigern's hall. For a moment he wondered about the winks that Hengist and Horsa had made to each other. Then he forgot about them and fell asleep.

As the sun came up he was given beer and bread to eat and some cheese and an apple for the journey. He was given a horse. Some of Hengist's men rode with him to his ship. At the last moment Hengist gave him a message for King Vortigern - Yes, they would all come and help fight the invading Picts and Scots. They would come soon and the payment should be as the king said in food and land.

The messenger rode away happily. King Vortigern would be pleased with him. Perhaps he would be given land as a reward and soon he would be important in the King's Council.

### Preparations

The village had never been so busy. Hengist sent messengers to all the nearby leaders inviting them to come with him to Britain. Horsa found supplies for their three boats and checked that the oars were in good repair.

They chose only the strongest and fittest men who came with swords, shields and helmets. They set off full of hope. There would be treasure and land. Soon their families would join them. It was all planned by Hengist and Horsa. The men were proud to go with such brave leaders.

*continued*

### Meeting King Vortigern

It had been easy. A few good battles and the Picts and Scots had run away. There was a victory feast. The men sat at the far end of King Vortigern's hall. They could see Hengist and Horsa and King Vortigern finishing the feast and talking together.

King Vortigern looked a good leader. His men talked about his wisdom and his bravery. In return Hengist's men praised him too. That was what happened at the end of a victory feast. Everyone was happy and friendly.

Before they went to sleep the whispers went round the hall. King Vortigern would keep the bargain. There would be land for all the fighters.

### Secret Winks

Hengist and Horsa shared out the land among their men. Then they called a meeting. They told all the men to send for their families and they winked!

The men understood. They all had very big families. Not just their wives and children but all their cousins too. There was plenty of land and King Vortigern's men were not trained and brave fighters.

The boats arrived just a few at a time. Soon there were lots of men. Hengist and Horsa went to King Vortigern. They said that they must have more land to give all the brave men who had fought against the Picts and Scots.

King Vortigern said he had kept his side of the bargain. The new men must go home. Hengist and Horsa said he was not honourable. He must give more land. King Vortigern refused.

### Enemies Ally

Hengist and Horsa were furious. They had been promised land for all the families and now there were men without land. Hengist and Horsa were blamed.

Quickly they joined up with the Picts and Scots. Together they attacked King Vortigern and his men. Hengist and Horsa won and they took more land for all their men. Then more men came in boats. They fought again and took more land. Each time they winked at each other. Soon they were very powerful.

# The story of King Raedwald and King Edwin adapted from Bede

*Ideas for using this material can be found on page 48*

One day the high King Raedwald of the East Angles had a visitor. It was King Edwin of Northumbria and he needed help. His kingdom had been taken by a man called Ethelfrith after a battle. King Raedwald said that Edwin could stay with him in safety.

Then Ethelfrith sent secret messengers to the high King Raedwald. He offered the high King treasure if he would murder Edwin. The high king refused.

Again Ethelfrith sent secret messengers. This time he offered still more treasure if the high king would give Edwin to the messengers. They would take him back to Northumbria as a captive. If the high king did not do this then Ethelfrith would come and attack him.

The high King began to think he would like all that treasure. Someone told Edwin about this and he was too scared to go to sleep. That night a stranger came to talk to Edwin. He promised to help Edwin win back Northumbria. In return Edwin promised to help the stranger in years to come. Suddenly the stranger vanished and Edwin knew he had been talking to a spirit.

Meanwhile the high king Raedwald told his queen about his plan to get all the treasure. She said he must not sell his friend Edwin for treasure. He was a great king and all his men would stop respecting him if he sold his friend.

The high king listened to the queen. He did not give Edwin to the messengers. He sent them back to Northumbria. Then he called for an army and made a surprise attack on Ethelfrith and killed him. Edwin was king of Northumbria again.

When King Raedwald died in AD625 Edwin became high king. One day he was sitting alone when the stranger came back to see him. He asked Edwin to become a Christian. Edwin kept his promise. He became a Christian and so did the people of Northumbria.